The Nitration Of Aniline And Certain Of Its Derivatives

Frederick Conrad Blanck

In the interest of creating a more extensive selection of rare historical book reprints, we have chosen to reproduce this title even though it may possibly have occasional imperfections such as missing and blurred pages, missing text, poor pictures, markings, dark backgrounds and other reproduction issues beyond our control. Because this work is culturally important, we have made it available as a part of our commitment to protecting, preserving and promoting the world's literature. Thank you for your understanding.

The Nitration of Aniline and Certain of Its Derivatives.

DISSERTATION

SUBMITTED TO THE BOARD OF UNIVERSITY STUDIES OF
THE JOHNS HOPKINS UNIVERSITY IN CONFORMITY
WITH THE REQUIREMENTS FOR THE DEGREE
OF DOCTOR OF PHILOSOPHY.

BY

FRED C. Conrad BLANCK.

1907

EASTON, PA.:
ESCHENBACH PRINTING COMPANY,
1908

TABLE OF CONTENTS.

Acknowledgment	4
Theoretical	5
Experimental	12
Summary of Results	29
Table	31
General Discussion of Results	32
Biographical	38

ACKNOWLEDGMENT.

The author takes pleasure in expressing his gratitude to President Remsen, Professor Morse, Professor Jones and Professor Matthews, for instruction received from them, and especially to Professor Tingle, under whose direction this investigation has been pursued, for guidance in the work and for his personal interest. Thanks are also due to Messrs. Cram, Morse, and Lovelace for assistance in the preparation of material.

Studies in Nitration. Nitration of Aniline and of Certain of Its *N*-Alkyl, *N*-Aryl and *N*-Acyl Derivatives.

Theoretical.

The fact that aniline cannot be directly nitrated and that, under ordinary conditions, nitric acid converts it into tarry matter, is usually accounted for by stating that the acid attacks the amino group more readily than the benzene nucleus.[1] Such an explanation cannot be accepted unreservedly, not only because it is devoid of experimental foundation, but also because of certain theoretical objections which may be urged against it. Among the latter may be mentioned the view, held by many chemists, that "substitution" in the nucleus is really preceded by addition or substitution in the side chain, if one be present, or addition in the nucleus itself, followed in each case by subsequent rearrangement. Further, the fact that, in general, the aromatic amine *nitrates* are usually stable, whereas, the *nitrites* are either highly unstable or altogether incapable of isolation suggests that nitrous acid may really be the active cause of the unfavorable result of direct nitration experiments. This view gains support from the well-known observations made in carrying out the diazo reaction; some resinous matter is always formed and it is apt to be the chief, or even the only tangible product of the experiment, unless the conditions are adjusted specially for each individual amine.

In view of these considerations, it appeared to me that it would be worth while to reinvestigate the direct nitration of aniline, employing conditions which should exclude nitrous acid as completely as possible from the materials employed, provision being also made for the speedy destruction or removal of any of this acid which might be formed during the course of the experiments.

Many careful and painstaking investigations have been carried out on the general phenomena of nitration. Much of this work has been done with the object of studying the effect of different atoms or complexes with respect to their influence on the position assumed by entering nitro groups.

[1] Vide, for example, Lassar-Cohn's "Application of Some General Organic Reactions," translated by J. Bishop Tingle, p. 3, *et. seq.*

As the result of these researches many "rules" have been promulgated by different chemists at various times. The most important conclusions are, perhaps, best summarized by Brown and Gibson, as follows:[1] "When a monobenzene derivative, C_6H_5X, is so treated as to give a dibenzene derivative, C_6H_4XY, it is well known that, as a rule, this dibenzene derivative is either (a) exclusively, or nearly so, a *meta* compound or (b) a mixture of *ortho* and *para* with none or very little *meta*; and that whether the case shall fall under (a) or (b) depends on the nature of the radicle X, and not at all, or only very slightly, on the nature of Y."

Blanksma explains the phenomena of nitration by supposing that there is "a direct and indirect introduction of the nitro group." In the former reaction the nitro group replaces hydrogen directly, whereas, in the latter a nitrate is formed primarily, which changes subsequently to the true nitro compound. Indirect substitution always gives *ortho* and *para* derivatives; direct substitution gives the three possible isomers with the *meta* derivative as the principal product. I shall refer to this point more fully later.

Although possessing some value, such rules are not very satisfactory, partly on account of vagueness and partly because they fail to take into account the formation of all three isomers in many cases. Moreover, on examining the literature carefully, it is found that many of the statements in it are contradictory. Instances of this will be found in the detailed references which I have made in connection with each compound studied by me.

Of the more recent work on the nitration of derivatives of benzene and aniline, it seems desirable to call attention to the investigations of Holleman,[2] who has attempted to determine, by careful and painstaking effort, the effect of relatively small quantities of water on the nature and quantity of the isomers formed. In subsequent papers[3] this author deals still further with the question of substitution in the benzene nucleus and the simultaneous formation of isomeric substitution products of benzene.

Other recent work which is of interest in this connection is that of Holdermann,[4] who has studied the influence of catalytic agents on sub-

[1] *J. Chem. Soc.*, 61, 367 (1892).
[2] *Ber.*, 39, 1607 (1906).
[3] *Centrabl.*, 1906, I, 457; 1906, I, 770; 1906, I, 773; *Rec. trav. chim.*, 25, 208.
[4] *Ber.*, 39, 1250 (1906).

stitution in the aromatic nucleus. The nitration of toluene yields a mixture of ortho and paramononitrotoluene, which, when the nitration is carried out in a mixture of nitric and sulphuric acids at 5° to 10°, consists of 59–60 per cent. of the *ortho* derivative. This yield was not changed by the presence of various catalyzers, such as reduced copper, copper nitrate, mercury, mercurous nitrate, mercuric sulphate, reduced nickel, cobalt nitrate and ammonium vanadate.

Francis,[1] in an interesting paper, pointed out the possibility of using benzoyl nitrate, $C_6H_5COONO_2$, as a new nitrating agent. His experiments show that, when nitrating with benzoyl nitrate, more orthonitro derivative is formed than para, the reactions in the case of anisole and phenetole yielding *theoretical* quantities of the orthonitro derivatives.

Experiments giving results similar to these were made by Pictet and Khotinsky,[2] who used acetyl nitrate, CH_3COONO_2, as their nitrating agent.

With this reagent almost theoretical yields of mononitro derivatives were obtained in all cases. In the substituted benzenes, the same tendency toward the formation of *o*-nitro derivatives, which Francis had previously pointed out, was noticed. Thus, toluene gave 88 per cent. of *o*-nitro and 12 per cent. of *p*-nitro derivative; phenol, 52 per cent. of *o*-nitro and 48 per cent. of *p*-nitro derivative; benzyl chloride, 60 per cent. of *o*-nitro and 40 per cent. of *p*-nitro derivative, while acetanilide gave 100 per cent. of *o*-nitro compound.

These results are of especial interest because the nitrating agents used by both Francis and Pictet necessarily insure the complete absence of water from the reacting substances at all stages of the experiments. Further reference will be made to them later.

In addition to my work on aniline itself, I desired to study, in a more detailed manner than had been done heretofore, the action of substituting groups on the process of nitration. With this, the further question was raised as to the influence of materials, other than nitric acid, which might be added to the reacting mixture. It has been shown, for example, that the use of a mixture of sulphuric and nitric acids does not simply act as a more powerful nitrating agent, by withdrawing the elements of water, but that the sulphuric acid exerts a directive[3] influence on the position assumed by the entering nitro group, in general;

[1] *Ber.*, **39**, 3798 (1906).
[2] *Ibid.*, **40**, 1163 (1907).
[3] Bishop Tingle and Blanck: *Am. Chem. Jour.*, **36**, 607.

this position is the *meta* one. This is seen in the case of methyl aniline,[1] ethylaniline[2] and dimethylaniline[3] and diethylaniline.[4] The results obtained by Reverdin[5] and his co-workers show, similarly, that, in the nitration of *p*-aminophenol and its derivatives in the presence of sulphuric acid, metanitro compounds are formed.

I thought it desirable to try to ascertain whether a similar directive influence could be established for other acids. A mixture of acetic and nitric acids has frequently been employed for nitrating purposes, the acetic acid having been regarded as an essentially indifferent solvent.

A few experiments have also been made by Orton[6] with nitric acid and acetic anhydride in acetic acid solution.

So far as I have been able to discover, no experiments have been carried out with nitrating mixtures of nitric acid and acids intermediate in strength between sulphuric and acetic acids, and I have, therefore, included this problem in my work. The choice of acids was necessarily rather limited. Obviously they had to be such as would not be acted on readily by nitric acid, and they had to be available in reasonably large quantity. I selected, eventually, anhydrous oxalic acid and trichloracetic acid. The former was chosen partly because it is dibasic, but chiefly because of its intermediate position in strength between the other two. It suffers from the disadvantage of sparing solubility in rather highly concentrated nitric acid, but it appeared to be worth while to carry out a sufficient number of experiments with it to discover if the quantity which did dissolve was sufficiently large to exert an appreciable influence on the nitration process. So far as my experiments permit of a conclusion being drawn, this does not appear to be the case. The results obtained by nitrating in the presence of oxalic acid appear to be essentially the same as those given by direct nitration.

Trichloracetic acid was chosen because it is, practically, the strongest acid which is available for use in any quantity. It may be convenient here to give the dissociation constants of these four acids, as the values afford an approximate indication of their relative strengths. For acetic

[1] *Centrabl.*, 1901, (I), 105.
[2] *Ber.*, **19**, 546 (1886).
[3] *Ibid.*, **19**, 198.
[4] *Ibid.*, **19**, 199.
[5] *Ibid.*, **39**, 125, 971, 2679, 3793.
[6] *J. Chem. Soc.*, **81**, 806.

acid, K = 0.0018; oxalic acid, K = 10.00; trichloracetic acid, K = 121.00; sulphuric acid, K = 130.0, approximately, by calculation.

A further point which influenced my choice of these acids was that they included a strong and a weak monobasic organic acid, a dibasic organic acid of medium strength, and a strong, dibasic, inorganic acid. It might be expected, therefore, that my results would throw light on the question as to whether the factors of the basicity or constitution of these admixed acids influenced the results of nitration, or whether the effect which they produced was due only to their strength. It will also be noticed that, in so far as "strength" is concerned, sulphuric and trichloracetic acids are in the same class[1] and should, therefore, permit of a conclusion being drawn as to the influence, if any, of the mono- or dibasicity of the admixed acid and of its organic or inorganic composition, $i.\ e.$, as to the specific influence of a carboxyl group.

Regarding the nature of the aniline derivatives to be employed, an inspection of the literature revealed the fact that N-substituted derivatives had been less worked with than those where substitution had taken place in the nucleus.

The compounds employed may be divided into the following classes:

A. Experiments with Aniline.

a. Nitration experiments.
b. Formation of aniline nitrate.

B. Aliphatic Compounds.

I.—*Alkyl Derivatives.*
   a. Monalkyl: 1. Methylaniline; 2. Ethylaniline.
   b. Dialkyl: 1. Dimethylaniline; 2. Diethylaniline.

II.—*Derivatives of Monobasic Acids.*
   1. Formanilide; 2. Acetanilide; 3. Trichloracetanilide; 4. Propanilide; 5. Stearanilide.

III.—*Derivatives of Dibasic Acids.*
   1. Oxanilic acid; 2. Oxanilide; 3. Succinanilic acid; 4. Succinanil; 5. Succinanilide; 6. Tartranilide.

IV.—*Derivatives of Tribasic Acids.*
   1. Citranilide; 2. Citrobianil.

[1] Cf. Kastle: *Am. Chem. Jour.*, **33**, 52 (1905).

C. Aromatic Compounds.

I.—*Aryl Derivatives*.
    1. Benzanilide; 2. Metabrombenzanilide; 3. Phenylsulphanilide;
    1. Diphenylamine; 2. Benzalaniline.

II.—*Derivatives of Monobasic Acids*.
    4. Orthotolylsulphanilide; 5. Phenylacetanilide; 6. Picranilide.

III.—*Derivatives of Dibasic Acids*.
    1. Phthalanilic acid; 2. Phthalanil.

I desired to avoid, as far as possible, the formation of polynitro derivatives, consequently the experiments were usually carried out at room temperatures. In cases where there was a considerable evolution of heat on mixing the substances, cooling with ice was resorted to. Sometimes the mixtures were surrounded by ice and salt during the whole time of an experiment. Occasionally, however, gentle warming was requisite to promote a reaction.

The experiments were carried out with the following reagents: 1. Nitric acid, sp. gr. = 1.46, containing 80 per cent. of HNO_3. 2. Nitric acid, sp. gr. = 1.46, with glacial acetic acid in the proportion 1.25 mols. of nitric acid to 4 mols. of acetic acid. 3. Nitric acid, sp. gr. = 1.46, and anhydrous oxalic acid in the proportion 1.25 mols. of nitric acid to 4 mols. of oxalic acid. 4. Nitric acid, sp. gr. = 1.46, and trichloracetic acid, in the proportion of 1.25 mols. of nitric acid to 4 mols. of trichloracetic acid. 5. Nitric acid, sp. gr. = 1.46, and concentrated sulphuric acid, sp. gr. = 1.83, containing about 92 per cent. of H_2SO_4, in the proportion of 1.25 mols. of nitric acid to 4 mols. of sulphuric acid. When the particular substance under investigation was soluble with difficulty, an excess over 4 mols. of sulphuric or acetic acid was employed. A few experiments were carried out with other solvents such, as acetic anhydride or carbon tetrachloride.

In all the experiments with aniline itself we used nitric acid which had been freed from dissolved oxides by means of a current of dry air. Oxidation during the experiment was avoided, as far as possible, by employing nitric acid of 99 per cent. concentration, made according to the method described by Morse.[1] Freshly distilled aniline was always used.

I carried out the experiments in platinum vessels, placed in a freezing mixture, so as to keep the temperature as low as possible, and took

[1] "Quantitative Analysis," p. 247.

care that the reagents were mixed gradually and stirred thoroughly; moreover, I operated in the presence of urea, in the hope that any nitrous acid which might be produced by the possible reduction of some of the nitric acid would be instantly decomposed by this reagent.

In some experiments, aniline nitrate was employed in place of aniline, so as to eliminate the heat of formation of this salt. In every case, however, it was found to be impossible to keep the temperature sufficiently low and, as soon as it rose, tarry, or carbonaceous products were formed. The result was identical whether the acid was added to the aniline or *vice versa*.

This series of experiments, Nos. 1 to 7, was, therefore, discontinued and another series, Nos. 8 to 14, undertaken in order to determine at what concentration of nitric acid the formation of aniline nitrate ceases and nitration—or charring—begins. The results demonstrated that any strength of acid could be used up to at least 75.33 per cent. of HNO_3 provided, in the case of the more concentrated acids (above 50 per cent.), that the mixture was cooled and excess of acid was avoided. Acids of 50.71 to 75.33 per cent. always gave, with aniline, the pink-colored solid compound described previously.[1]

With acids above 75.33 per cent. of HNO_3, charring took place rather quickly, although the aniline was in considerable excess. I believe, however, that this is due to the impossibility of preventing local superheating, *i. e.*, to the action of the concentrated acid, at a relatively high temperature, on aniline nitrate. Be this as it may, it is certain that, with acids containing up to 75.33 per cent. of HNO_3, any charring which may be brought about is due to an attack on aniline nitrate and not to one of free aniline. I emphasize this rather obvious fact in order to contrast it with the behavior of aniline towards a mixture of nitric and sulphuric acids, in which the latter is in considerable excess. In these circumstances, as is well known, nitration proceeds smoothly, because, as it is usually expressed, the sulphuric acid "protects" the amino group. Surely, however the amino group is equally well "protected" in the nitrate, $C_6H_5NH_3NO_3$, as in the sulphate, $C_6H_5NH_3SO_4H$, and the excess of concentrated sulphuric acid which is present must abstract so much water from the nitric acid as to make it of a higher concentration than 75.33 per cent. of HNO_3. The only very obvious difference in the conditions of the experiments, so far as I can see, is in that which governs

[1] Bishop Tingle and Blanck: *Am. Chem. Jour.*, 36, 607 (1906).

the *temperature*. In the experiment with sulphuric acid all the materials are in solution and the "heat of nitration," as it may be termed, is instantaneously absorbed and diffused throughout the large volume of comparatively indifferent sulphuric acid, whereas, in my experiments with aniline nitrate and nitric acid, I had to reply on the relatively slow, inefficient and clumsy mechanical means of stirring and external cooling to neutralize this heat.

Of my experiments with the derivatives of aniline, practically every one has been repeated three or four times; indeed, some of them have been carried out eight or ten times, in order to verify a result, to obtain a larger quantity of product, or for the purpose of determining the influence of some variable factor, such as temperature, concentration, etc.

I realize very fully the magnitude of the problems which I have attacked and I regard the present results as constituting merely a preliminary survey of the field; there is a mass of detailed work which must necessarily be carried out before the subject can be regarded as being at all well known.

Experimental.

A. a. Experiments on the Nitration of Aniline. (Nos. 1–7.) *Experiments with Aniline and Concentrated Nitric Acid in Presence of Urea.* 1. 23.2 grams aniline (1 mol.), 32 grams nitric acid (2 mols.) and 75 grams urea. The vessel containing the aniline was kept immersed in a salt and ice bath and constantly stirred. A small quantity of the urea was added and then the nitric acid gradually, *drop by drop*, with further additions of small quantities of urea. It was found impossible to keep the temperature low, and there was consqently a violent decomposition of the nitric acid with a copious evolution of nitrogen peroxide; the aniline became tarry and, finally, only a charred mass remained in the vessel.

2. The procedure was the same as in the preceding experiment except that the nitric acid was stirred and aniline was added to the acid. Here, again, it was impossible to control the temperature, with the result that the nitric acid decomposed and the contents of the beaker took fire, burning fiercely even at the very low initial temperature.

Experiment with Aniline Nitrate. 3. 39 grams aniline nitrate (1 mol.), made by treating freshly distilled aniline with dilute nitric acid, 48 grams nitric acid (3 mols.), and 7.5 grams urea. The procedure was the same as in the preceding experiments. On the completion of the reaction, the mixture was poured into twice its volume of ice-water and filtered. This gave a red liquid and a black precipitate. Each was treated with sodium carbonate but in neither case could any definite compound be isolated.

The next experiments were taken with a view to study the possible effect of various solvents on the nitration. Carbon tetrachloride, acetic anhydride, and a mixture of the two were employed.

Experiments on the Use of Carbon Tetrachloride and Acetic Anhydride as Solvents.

4. 10 Grams aniline (1 mol.), 10.1 grams nitric acid (1.5 mols.) and 100 cc. carbon tetrachloride. The aniline was dissolved in the carbon tetrachloride, and the nitric acid added drop by drop to the cooled solution. A reddish precipitate was obtained and at the same time a bright blue coloration was noticed on the side of the vessel. Part of precipitate was taken out, washed with alcohol and dried over-night on a porous plate. It was colored reddish-white and melted and decomposed at 207–209°. After the mixture had stood twenty-four hours longer, the melting point of the product was 190–194° and the color had changed to green. Aniline nitrate itself melts at 195–197° and the mixture of the reaction product with aniline nitrate melted at 192–195°, thus indicating that the substance was only aniline nitrate. The rest of the original precipitate was allowed to remain in the vessel in contact with the acid and after a time it charred. The carbon tetrachloride solution was filtered and evaporated, but nothing remained except a tar.

5. 10 Grams aniline (1 mol.), 10.11 grams nitric acid (1.5 mols.), and 109.1 grams acetic anhydride (10 mols.). Nitric acid and part of the acetic anhydride were carefully mixed and well cooled and the mixture added drop by drop to the solution of aniline in the rest of the anhydride. The product of the reaction was colored red and gave a red solution. It was stirred continually and allowed to remain in the ice bath 1¼ hours. On pouring into water a flocculent, yellow precipitate was obtained. This was extracted with benzene, from which a yellow product crystallized out, melting at 89–92°.

6. 10 Grams aniline (1 mol.), 10.11 grams nitric acid (1.5 mols.), 100 cc. carbon tetrachloride, and 19 grams acetic anhydride. The aniline was dissolved in carbon tetrachloride and the cold mixture of the nitric acid and acetic anhydride was added, drop by drop. A dark red, crystalline product was obtained. This was dissolved in water and neutralized with sodium carbonate. On standing, aniline, identified by testing with bleaching powder solution, separated out.

The next experiment was made to test the effect of *nascent nitric acid*.

7. 10 Grams aniline (1 mol.), 105 grams sulphuric acid (10 mols.), and 16.2 grams potassium nitrate (1.5 mols.). The aniline and sulphuric acid were mixed and powdered potassium nitrate was slowly added. The solution and precipitate obtained on pouring into ice-water were both colored dark green, which, on standing, changed to red, the precipitate then being colored greenish-black. This was filtered off and the filtrate extracted with ether, but on evaporation of the ether nothing but a tar remained. The precipitate was insoluble in ether, but dissolved in alcohol, which, however, on evaporation left only a tarry residue.

(b) *Experiments on the Formation of Aniline Nitrate.* (Nos. 8–14).

8. 20 Grams of aniline were treated with nitric acid which contained 29.38 per cent. of HNO_3. Reaction took place readily on gentle heating. When the concentration of the solution was sufficient, aniline nitrate crystallized out. In the latter stages of the reaction, the addition of the nitric acid caused a pink coloration of the crystals, which disappeared after a time.

9. Nitric acid of sp. gr. 1.250, containing 39.82 per cent. of HNO_3, was used. The phenomena were identical with those described in Experiment 8.

10. Nitric acid, of sp. gr. 1.320, containing 50.71 per cent. of HNO_3, was used. The reaction took place more readily than in the preceding experiments and with an increase in the color phenomena. The crystals also were somewhat more finely divided. There was a slight fuming and darkening of the aniline with *almost immediate* formation of crystals. The liquid had a reddish-brown color which disappeared on standing.

11. Nitric acid of sp. gr. 1.350, containing 55.79 per cent. of HNO_3, was used. A reaction took place in the cold with immediate formation of crystals. The pink coloration assumed by crystals on each addition of nitric acid was especially noticeable. As in the preceding experiments, this color gradually disappeared.

12. Nitric acid of sp. gr. 1.375, containing 60.30 per cent. of HNO_3, was used. Here, again, aniline nitrate was formed with the accompanying color phenomena.

13. Nitric acid of sp. gr. 1.400, containing 65.30 per cent. of HNO_3, was used. The aniline was added to the acid, which was cooled in a salt and ice mixture. In this case the product was tarry. The experiment was repeated in a platinum dish, under the same conditions; no tar was found, the production of aniline nitrate being complete. On standing at the room temperature, decomposition set in after a time.

14. Aniline was treated with nitric acid of sp. gr. 1.4425, containing 75.33 per cent. of HNO_3, in a platinum vessel cooled by a salt and ice mixture. Here the color phenomena were again well marked. Exposure for a short time to the room temperature sufficed to cause the decomposition of the aniline nitrate.

B. I. Alkyl Compounds.

a. Monalkyl. 1. *Experiments with Methylaniline* (Nos. 15–19). As will be seen from the reference given below, a considerable amount of work has been done by many chemists, on the ortho-,[1] meta-,[2] and paramononitro[3] derivatives of this compound.

15. *Methylaniline, nitric acid and acetic acid.* In this and the following experiments unless otherwise stated, the nitrating agents described on p. 1400 were used. For each molecule of the aniline derivative, 1.25 molecules of nitric acid and 4 molecules of glacial acetic, anhydrous oxalic, trichloracetic or sulphuric acid, respectively, were employed.

The methylaniline and acetic acid were mixed while the latter was cooled. The nitric acid was then added, drop by drop. The solution became colored dark green. On pouring into water no precipitate was obtained and the aqueous solution was also colored green. It was extracted with ether; on evaporating the latter a tar remained. Experiments had previously been tried in which the reaction was allowed to take place at room temperature and others where the solution was warmed on the water bath; the time of standing was also varied, but in all cases tars were formed.

[1] *J. prakt. Chem.* [2], **41**, 164; [2], **46**, 565; *Ber.*, **27**, 369; **27**, 378; **31**, 2927. *Monatsh.*, **19**, 634; *Rec. trav. chim.*, **21**, 272; *Centrabl.*, **1902**, II, 514.

[2] *Ber.*, **19**, 548; *Centrabl.*, **1901**, I, 105; *Ann.*, **327**, 112; *Centrabl.*, **1903**, I, 1213.

[3] *Bull. soc. chim.*, **53**, 775; *Ber.*, **27**, 370, 3791; 520; **31**, 2529, 2926, **33**, 113; *Rec. trav. chim.*, **21**, 270; *Centrabl.*, **1902**, II, 513.

16. Nitric and oxalic acids.
17. Nitric and trichloracetic acids.
18. Nitric acid alone.

In all these experiments the products were tars.

19. Nitrating methylaniline in the presence of sulphuric acid gives m-nitromethylaniline.[1]

2. *Experiments with Ethylaniline* (Nos. 20–24). The ortho-,[2] meta-,[3] and paramononitro[4] derivatives of this compound have been far less extensively investigated than those of methylaniline.

Nitration in presence of acetic acid (Ex. 20), oxalic acid (Ex. 21), trichloracetic acid (Ex. 22) and with nitric acid alone (Ex. 23) gave only tars. Paranitroethylaniline is formed by the action of a mixture of nitric and sulphuric acids[5] (Ex. 24).

b. *Dialkyl.* 1. *Experiments with Dimethylaniline* (Nos. 25–30). As shown below, the ortho-,[6] meta-,[7] and paranitro[8] derivatives of this compound have all been investigated to some extent.

25. Nitrating dimethylaniline in the presence of sulphuric acid gives m-nitrodimethylaniline.[9]

26. Nitratino dimethylaniline in the presence of glacial acetic acid yields p-nitrodimethylaniline.[10]

27. *Dimethylaniline and Nitric Acid.* No matter how the conditions of nitration were varied, a tar was always produced.

28. *Dimethylaniline, Nitric Acid and Trichloracetic Acid.* Resinous substances were formed.

29. *Dimethylaniline, Nitric Acid and Oxalic Acid.* The dimethylaniline and oxalic acid were added at a low temperature, which, however, could not be controlled by the rather primitive means at my command, consequently charring took place. The addition of the mixture of aniline and oxalic acid to cooled nitric acid gave similar results. Then a mixture of oxalic and nitric acids was used; it was carefully cooled and dimethylaniline was added to it *drop by drop*. It was found best to work in small quantities and to have both the aniline and acid mixture cooled. No tar was formed under these conditions.

Experiments were also tried with nitric acid of different concentrations. All of the higher concentration caused the production of tar, but this was not formed by

[1] *Centrabl.*, **1901**, I, 105.
[2] *J. pr. Chem.* [2], **41**, 163.
[3] *Ber.*, **19**, 546.
[4] *Ibid.*, **16**, 31; **17**, 267; **19**, 149.
[5] *Ibid.*, **19**, 546.
[6] *Monatsh.*, **19**, 635.
[7] *Ber.*, **19**, 198, 1944; **27**, 1932; **30**, 2931; *Ann.*, **377**, 112; *Centrabl.*, **1903**, I, 1213; *Ber.*, **37**, 2616; *Centrabl.*, **1904**, II, 517.
[8] *Ber.*, **8**, 620; **10**, 761; **12**, 529; **14**, 2176; **15**, 1234; **27**, 379; *Bull. soc. chim.* [3], **23**, 25; *Ber.*, **32**, 1896.
[9] *Ibid.*, **19**, 198.
[10] *Ibid.*, **10**, 761; **14**, 2176.

the use of acid containing 21 per cent. HNO_3. On pouring the product of the reaction into water, filtering, and boiling the precipitate with alcohol and animal charcoal, beautiful yellow needles melting at 80–82° were obtained.

30. *Dimethylaniline (1 mol.), Nitric Acid (1.25 mols.), Oxalic Acid (4 mols.) and Acetic Acid (excess over 4 mols.).* The dimethylaniline and oxalic acid were ground together and dissolved in acetic acid. Then nitric acid was added and the product allowed to stand for a time. On pouring the acid liquid into water a greenish-yellow precipitate came down. This was filtered, dried, and then extracted with alcohol, from which p-nitrodimethylaniline crystallized out in beautiful yellowish-green needles melting at 162°–165°.

2. *Experiments with Diethylaniline* (Nos. 31–35). Only the meta-[1] and paranitro[2] derivatives of this compound appear to be known.

31. By nitrating diethylaniline in the presence of sulphuric acid, m-nitrodiethylaniline and some p-nitrodiethylaniline are obtained[3]. Nitration in the presence of acetic acid (Ex. 32), oxalic acid (Ex. 33), trichloracetic acid (Ex. 34) and nitric acid alone (Ex. 35) yielded only tarry or carbonaceous materials.

II. Aryl Compounds.

1. *Experiments with Diphenylamine* (Nos. 36–41). Considerable work has been carried out on the nitro derivatives of this substance but much still remains to be done. The ortho-[4] and paramononitro[5] derivatives have been prepared but, apparently, the meta compound is not known. Of the dinitro substitution products, the disymmetrical meta compound does not appear to have been isolated. On the other hand, several chemists have investigated the disymmetrical ortho-,[6] the disymmetrical-para,[7] and the 2,4-dinitro[8] derivatives.

36. *Diphenylamine, Nitric Acid (2.5 mols.) and Sulphuric Acid (excess over 4 mols.).* The sulphuric acid and diphenylamine were mixed and cooled; nitric acid was then added, drop by drop, which developed the well-known blue-purple color. The nitric acid was partially decomposed and some tar was also formed. On pouring the reaction product into water, a brown precipitate was obtained.

37. *Diphenylamine, Nitric Acid (2.5 mols.) and Acetic Acid.* A small quantity of a brown precipitate was obtained. This was boiled with water. The residue insoluble in water was then extracted for some hours with alcohol in a Soxhlet apparatus. On standing, yellow-green crystals separated. They melted below 60°, thus indicating that they did not consist of a nitro derivative.

[1] *Ber.*, **19**, 199, 550.
[2] *Monatsh.*, **4**, 293; *Ber.*, **19**, 199.
[3] *Ibid.*, **19**, 199.
[4] *Ber.*, **23**, 1840; **24**, 3796; *Centrabl.*, 1898, II, 342; *Frdl.*, III, 46; *Centrabl.* 1899, II, 961.
[5] *Ber.*, **11**, 757; **15**, 827; **31**, 590; *Ann.*, **132**, 167; *Centrabl.*, 1899, II, 961.
[6] *Ber.*, **11**, 759; **12**, 1400; **15**, 829; **28**, 2976; **31**, 580; *Ann.*, **132**, 167.
[7] *Ber.*, **11**, 759; **12**, 1400; **15**, 828; **31**, 580; **31**, 2535; *Ann.*, **132**, 167.
[8] *J. pr. Chem.* [1], **108**, 320; [2], **1**, 175; *Ber.*, **3**, 128; **9**, 977; **31**, 2536; *Bull. soc. chim.*, **30**, 5; *Ann.*, **215**, 363; *J. pr. Chem.* [2], **68**, 254; *Centrabl.*, 1903, II, 1064.

The experiment was then repeated at the temperature of the water bath. No precipitate was obtained on pouring the reaction product into water. The solution was colored red.

38. *Diphenylamine and Nitric Acid (excess over 2.5 mols.).* A reddish yellow precipitate was obtained. This was extracted with xylene, from which yellow crystals were deposited melting at 190°–194°.

39. *Diphenylamine, Nitric Acid (excess over 2.5 mols.) and Oxalic Acid.* A brownish yellow precipitate was obtained.

40. *Diphenylamine, Nitric Acid (2.5 mols.) and Trichloracetic Acid.* Diphenylamine and trichloracetic acid were ground together and nitric acid added, drop by drop, to the well-cooled mixture. After each addition of nitric acid there was a violent reaction with evolution of nitrogen peroxide. On pouring the product immediately into water a black tar separated out, leaving a brownish green solution.

41. *Diphenylamine, Nitric Acid (2.5 mols.) and Trichloacetic Acid.* Diphenylamine and trichloracetic acid were ground together and then acetic anhydride was added. This mixture was cooled and nitric acid gradually dropped in. On pouring the product into water, a tar separated.

2. *Experiments with Benzalaniline.* The meta-[1] and the paranitro[2] derivatives have been prepared from the corresponding nitranilines, but the ortho compound does not appear to have been obtained. My own experiments with this substance were only of a preliminary nature. They resulted, always, in the production of benzaldehyde and aniline, consequently they were not carried further and it is unnecessary to give them in any detail.

The conditions employed in my experiments with *N*-acyl derivatives of aniline were similar to those described above (p. 10). Unless otherwise stated, I used, with each molecule of the aniline compound, 1.25 molecules of nitric acid and 4 molecules of glacial acetic, anhydrous oxalic, trichloracetic or sulphuric acid, respectively. The nitric acid had sp. gr. = 1.46 and contained 80 per cent. of HNO_3; the sulphuric acid had sp. gr. = 1.83 and contained about 92 per cent. of H_2SO_4.

B. Aliphatic Compounds.

1. *Experiments with Formanilide* (Nos. 42–46).—The ortho-[3] meta-[4] and paranitro[5] derivatives of this compound have all been prepared, although their investigation has been far from exhaustive.

42. *Formanilide, Nitric Acid and Sulphuric Acid.* The anilide was added to the sulphuric acid and the mixture then cooled before the addition of the nitric acid, which was added drop by drop. After standing at room temperature about ten minutes,

---

[1] *Jahres. d. Chem.*, 1870, 760; *Monatsh.*, 9, 697; *Ber.*, 31, 2604.
[2] *Ber.*, 25, 2503; *Monatsh.*, 9, 697; *Ber.*, 34, 833; 35, 990; *Centrabl.*, 1902 (1), 870.
[3] *Ann.*, 209, 369; *Z. physik. Chem.*, 23, 459.
[4] *Am. Chem. J.*, 8, 346; *Z. physik. Chem.*, 23, 460.
[5] *Am. Chem. J.*, 8, 346; *Z. physik. Chem.*, 23, 460.

the reaction product was poured into ice-water and gave a brown precipitate, which was filtered off and dried. It was dissolved in boiling water, from which an orange-yellow precipitae came down. It melted at 187–192°. The substance was treated with boiling ligroin and the insoluble portion was dissolved in alcohol. The ligroin extract, on cooling, deposited a yellow, amorphous product which, when hydrolyzed with aqueous potassium hydroxide, gave p-nitraniline (m. p. 146–147°). The alcoholic solution deposited beautiful, brown needles melting at 151–154°.

43. *Formanilide, Nitric Acid and Acetic Acid.* Formanilide was dissolved in acetic acid and nitric acid added gradually. After standing for $1\frac{1}{2}$ hours the reaction product, was poured into water giving a red solution but no precipitate. This solution was then extracted with ether, which dissolved some of the red substance; on evaporating off the ether, no nitro derivative could be isolated from the residue. My earlier experiments had failed on account of the mixtures being allowed to stand too long. An experiment was also tried, using monochloracetic acid instead of glacial acetic acid, but only a tar was formed.

44. *Formanilide, Nitric Acid (excess over 1.25 mols.), and Oxalic Acid.* Formanilide and oxalic acid were ground together and added carefully to well cooled nitric acid. After a few minutes' standing at room temperature the material was poured into water; a yellow precipitate came down and the solution was also colored yellow. On further standing of the water solution, its color and also that of the precipitate became dark brown.

45. *Formanilide, Nitric Acid (excess over 1.25 mols.), and Trichloracetic Acid.* Formanilide and trichloracetic acid were ground together and added gradually to a well cooled excess of nitric acid. After standing a few minutes at room temperature, the reaction product was poured into water; it gave a small quantity of oil which, on further standing, became tarry.

46. The direct nitration of formanilide yields p-nitroformanilide.[1]

2. *Experiments with Acetanilide* (Nos. 47–51).—The ortho-,[2] meta-[3] and paranitro[4] derivatives of this compound have, of course, been investigated by many chemists. Some of the more interesting recent work has been referred to above (p. 7).

47. *Acetanilide, Nitric Acid and Sulphuric Acid.* The acetanilide was dissolved in a portion of the sulphuric acid. The nitric and the remainder of the sulphuric acid were carefully mixed and then added gradually to the solution of acetanilide. After standing several hours, the liquid was poured into ice-water; a yellow precipitate was obtained. This was recrystallized from hot water and proved to be m-nitracetanilide, m. p. 139–141°.

48. *Acetanilide, Nitric Acid and Trichloracetic Acid.* Acetanilide and trichlor-

[1] *Am. Chem. J.*, **8**, 346.

[2] *Ber.*, **9**, 775; **19**, 336; *Jahres. d. Chem.*, 1875, 344; *Ann.*, **209**, 352; **311**, 107.

[3] *Ann.*, **165**, 183; *J. prakt. Chem.* [2], **52**, 230; *Gazz. chim. ital.*, **24** (I), 446; *Am. Chem. J.*, **17**, 612; **18**, 87; **19**, 682; *Ber.*, **19**, 336; **31**, 661; *Bull. soc. chim.*, **53**, 778.

[4] *Z. Chem.*, 1871, 202; *Ann., Jahres. d. Chem.*, 1875, 344; 1677, 684; *Ann.*, **197**, 83; *Ber.*, **5**, 920; **9**, 775; **17**, 262; **19**, 336; *J. prakt. Chem.* [2], **52**, 233.

acetic acid were ground together in a mortar and nitric acid added to the mixture. It was allowed to remain an hour, after which time the reaction took place violently and the product decomposed. On repeating the experiment and cooling the vessel with water, a green-colored substance was obtained after seven hours' standing. It was poured into water, which caused the formation of a yellow precipitate and an oily green liquid. On filtering, the residue was colored brownish-black. This was partially soluble in hot water, from which an orange-colored compound separated out on cooling. It proved to be p-acetanilide, m. p. 205–207°.

49. *Acetanilide, Nitric Acid and Oxalic Acid.* Oxalic acid and acetanilide were ground together and added, little by little, to nitric acid cooled by means of salt and ice. When about two-fifths of the mixture had been added, decomposition took place. The reaction product was immediately poured into ice-water and a yellow precipitate was obtained which was recrystallized from hot water. It proved to be p-nitroacetanilide, m. p. 207–210°.

50. The direct nitration of acetanilide yields a mixture of ortho- and paranitroacetanilide.[1]

51. *Acetanilide, Nitric Acid and Acetic Acid.* Acetanilide was dissolved in acetic acid and the nitric acid added gradually. The solution became colored green. After standing some time, it was poured into ice-water and a white precipitate was obtained. This was then filtered off and recrystallized from water. It proved to be unchanged acetanilide, m. p. 112°–114°.

3. *Experiments with Trichloracetanilide* (Nos. 52–56).—Only the ortho[2] and paranitro[3] derivatives of this compound appear to have been described in the literature, consequently it has not been possible for me to identify the products which I have obtained. The reaction mixtures were allowed to stand for some time and poured into water. The results of the five experiments may be summarized as follows:

52. *Nitric and sulphuric acids* gave a dark yellow compound.
53. *Nitric and acetic acids* gave a yellowish white compound.
54. *Nitric and oxalic acids* gave a yellow amorphous substance.
55. *Nitric acid alone* gave a substance which was extracted with boiling water; a small quantity of a grayish-white material melting at 144.5–146.5° was obtained from the aqueous extract. The insoluble residue separated from alcohol in the form of a white, amorphous product, melting at 137–142°.
56. *Nitric and trichloracetic acids* yielded a light pink colored compound.

4. *Experiments with Propanilide* (Nos. 57–61).—The orthonitro derivative of this compound has been described,[4] but I have been unable to find any record of the preparation of the two isomers. Propanilide was prepared with great ease by treating propionyl chloride (1 mol.) with

[1] *Ber.*, 9, 775; *Jahres. d. Chem.*, 1875, 344; *Ann.*, 197, 83.
[2] *Ber.*, 40, 1735 (1907).
[3] *Ibid.*, 27, 1250; 40, 1735.
[4] *Am. Chem. J.*, 6, 172.

aniline (2.1 mols.) in benzene solution, at the ordinary temperature. The benzene was then evaporated off and the residue washed successively with water, dilute alkali and finally again with water. Subsequently it was recrystallized from alcohol.

57. *Nitric and sulphuric acids* gave a yellow flocculent product. The portion of it soluble in water was yellow and amorphous and melted at 150–160°. Alcohol extracted from the residue a yellowish red compound, melting at 189–192°.

58. *Nitric and acetic acids* gave a light brown product. From boiling water a grayish white compound was deposited, melting at 110–112°. Alcohol extracted a crystalline substance with a mother-of-pearl luster, melting at 100–104°.

59. *Nitric acid alone* yielded a brownish yellow, amorphous material. From boiling water a yellowish white substance was deposited melting at 100–101.5°.

60. *Nitric and oxalic acids* formed a yellow product.

61. *Nitric and trichloracetic acids* yielded a brown oil.

5. *Experiments with Stearanilide* (Nos. 62–66).—A careful search through the literature has failed to show me the record of the preparation of any mononitro derivative of this compound.

62. *Nitric and sulphuric acids* gave a yellow oil.

63. *Nitric and acetic acids* yielded a white soapy mass.

64. *Nitric and oxalic acids* formed a greenish white, soapy material, which became yellow when dry.

65. *Nitric acid alone* gave a greenish white precipitate which was yellow when dry.

66. *Nitric and trichloracetic acids* gave a product similar to that obtained in 65.

C. Aromatic Compounds.

II. Derivatives of Monobasic Acids.

1. *Experiments with Benzanilide* (Nos. 67–72).—As would be expected, a considerable number of chemists have investigated the ortho-,[1] meta-[2] and paranitro[3] derivatives of this compound.

67. *Benzanilide, Nitric Acid and Sulphuric Acid.* Benzanilide was dissolved in sulphuric acid, and nitric acid added to the well cooled mixture. After standing twenty-four hours, the reaction product was poured into water. At first, an oily layer separated, but this changed, later, to a green, flocculent precipitate. It was filtered off, dried and dissolved in hot alcohol. On cooling, a greenish white material was deposited. After being again recrystallized from hot alcohol it melted at 196–197°, thus proving to be *p*-nitrobenzanilide.

68. *Benzanilide, Nitric Acid and Acetic Acids* (*excess over 4 mols.*). Benzanilide was dissolved in an excess of acetic acid, and nitric acid added in the usual manner.

[1] *Ann.*, 208, 301; *Z. physik. Chem.*, 30, 539.
[2] *Ber.*, 7, 498; 10, 1078; 10, 1716; *Ann.*, 208, 297.
[3] *Ber.*, 7, 463; 7, 1315; 9, 774; 10, 1708; *Ann.*, 208, 294.

After standing over night, reaction did not seem to have taken place, so the temperature was raised gradually. At about 90°, the action appeared to be complete. On pouring into ice-water, a yellow, flocculent precipitate came down and also some blackish brown product. The yellow precipitate was dried and dissolved in alcohol, and the crystals obtained from alcohol were recrystallized from chloroform. They melted at 151–155°, which proved them to be m-nitrobenzanilide.

69. *Benzanilide, Nitric Acid and Oxalic Acid.* Benzanilide and oxalic acid were ground together and then dissolved in the least possible quantity of acetic acid. This solution was now treated with nitric acid at the room temperature. The mixture was then heated for a time and afterwards allowed to stand over-night, the reaction product being finally poured into water. A greenish-white precipitate separated out. This precipitate was extracted with ether and the residue insoluble in ether was dissolved in alcohol, from which a slate-colored compound came down. It melted at 154–155.5°, which proved it to be m-nitrobenzanilide.

70. *Nitric and oxalic acids* gave a greenish white precipitate.
71. *Nitric and trichloracetic acids* yielded a green precipitate.
72. The direct nitration of benzanilide forms a mixture of ortho-, meta- and paranitrobenzanilide.[1]

2. *Experiments with Metabrombenzanilide* (Nos. 73–77).—I have failed to find a record of the preparation of any nitranilide of m-brombenzoic acid.

73. *Nitric and sulphuric acids* gave a yellow substance.
74. *Nitric and acetic acids* yielded a pale yellow compound melting at 128–134°.
75. *Nitric acid alone* gave a yellow material.
76. *Nitric and oxalic acids* formed a bright yellow substance.
77. *Nitric and trichloracetic acids* gave a yellowish white compound.

3. *Experiments with Penylsulphanilide* (Nos. 78–82).—The ortho-,[2] meta-,[3] and paranitroanilides[4] of phenylsulphonic acids are all known.

78. *Nitric and acetic acids* gave a yellow precipitate.
79. *Nitric and oxalic acids* yielded a tar.
80. *Nitric acid alone* also gave a tar.
81. *Nitric and trichloracetic acids* gave an orange-yellow precipitate.
82. *Nitric and sulphuric acids* formed a substance which produced a red solution when the acid liquid was poured into water.

4. *Experiments with o-Tolylsulphanilide* (Nos. 83–87).—None of the nitranilides of o-tolylsulphanilides appear to have been prepared.

83. *o-Tolylsulphanilide, Nitric Acid and Sulphuric Acid* (excess over 4 mols.). The anilide was dissolved in an excess of sulphuric acid and nitric acid was added. After

[1] *Ann.*, 208, 292.
[2] *Ber.*, 16, 594; *Ann.*, 221, 16.
[3] *Ibid.*, 16, 595.
[4] *Ibid.*, 16, 595.

standing 24 hours, the reaction product was heated on the water bath for 6 hours. On pouring into water, the solution was colored yellowish red and the precipitate brownish yellow. The latter was boiled with water, and the insoluble residue boiled with alcohol and filtered. On cooling, fine, reddish yellow needles which melted at 117–131°, separated out. The residue, insoluble in alcohol, was boiled with benzene and the portion insoluble in this solvent was dissolved in nitrobenzene from which a white, amorphous substance was deposited. It softened at 180° and melted completely at 228°.

84. *Nitric and acetic acids* gave a yellow material. From this boiling water extracted a tar. The residue, when treated with alcohol, gave yellow crystals melting at 89–93°.

85. *Nitric and oxalic acids* yielded a yellow substance.

86. *Nitric acid alone* gave results similar to 8.5.

87. *Nitric and trichloracetic acids* formed a brown tar.

5. *Experiments with Phenylacetanilide* (Nos. 88–92).—There appears to be no record of the preparation of any nitranilide of phenylacetic acid.

88. *Nitric and sulphuric acid* gave a yellow amorphous material.

89. *Nitric and oxalic acids* yielded a brownish yellow substance and a red tar.

90. *Nitric acid alone* gave a yellowish white compound.

91. *Nitric and acetic acids* formed a white flocculent substance.

92. *Nitric and trichloracetic acids* gave a yellow compound.

6. *Experiments with Picranilide* (Nos. 93–97).—The ortho-,[1] meta-,[2] and paranitranilides[3] of picric acid have been investigated by several chemists.

93. *Picranilide, Nitric Acid and Sulphuric Acid (excess over 4 mols.).* Picranilide was dissolved in sulphuric acid, and nitric acid added at the room temperature. After standing over-night and pouring into water, a brown precipitate was obtained. This was filtered off and the filtrate extracted with ether. On evaporating the ether, a red, tarry mass remained. The crude precipitate was boiled with water, from which a very small amount of a greenish-yellow precipitate was extracted. It softens at 170° then melts completely and chars at 198°.

94. *Picranilide, Nitric Acid and Acetic Acid (excess over 4 mols.).* Picranilide was dissolved in acetic acid on the water bath. Nitric acid was added. and the mixture heated several hours. On pouring into water, a bright yellow precipitate came down. The crude precipitate was boiled with water and the residue was extracted with alcohol. A small amount of a red precipitate separated from the latter solution. It melted at 144–147°. The residue, insoluble in alcohol, was then extracted with benzene, from which a yellow compound melting at 155–159° was deosited. The residue, insoluble in benzene, was colored lemon-yellow and melted at 176–179°.

95. *Picranilide, Nitric Acid and Trichloracetic Acid.* Picranilide and trichloracetic acid were ground together and nitric acid added at the room temperature. After

[1] *Ber.*, **33**, 431.
[2] *Ibid.*, **7**, 1249; **33**, 431.
[3] *Ibid.*, **7**, 1249; **33**, 432.

standing over-night, the solution was poured into water; this produced a reddish yellow precipitate. It was boiled with water, and the residue was extracted with alcohol, from which crystals separated. They melted and decomposed at 155–157°. The residue, insoluble in boiling alcohol, was completely soluble in benzene; from this solution a product was obtained which melted and charred at 151–158°.

96. *Picranilide, Nitric Acid (excess over 1.25 mols.), and Oxalic Acid.* Picranilide and oxalic acid were ground together and added gradually to nitric acid at the room temperature. There was a slight warming and a small evolution of nitrogen peroxide. After standing for a few minutes the solution became red and thick. On adding it to water, a bright yellow compound was precipitated.

97. *Picranilide and Nitric Acid (excess over 1.25 mols.).* Picranilide was added to the nitric acid gradually at the room temperature. After standing some time it was poured into water, when a yellow precipitate came down. The crude precipitate was boiled with water, from which, on cooling, a small amount of yellowish-red, tarry matter was deposited. The residue, insoluble in boiling water, was then extracted with alcohol, from which solution a voluminous orange-red compound was obtained. It melted and decomposed at 160–162°. The residue, insoluble in boiling alcohol, was then extracted with benzene. The solution deposited slender, yellow crystals melting at 165–168°. The residue, insoluble in boiling benzene, consisted of a fine, yellow powder which melted and decomposed at 193–203°.

III. Derivatives of Dibasic Acids.

1. *Experiments with Oxanilic Acid* (Nos. 98–102).—The ortho-[1] and paranitro[2] derivatives of this compound are known and L. Weiss[3] has prepared the ethyl ester of the meta isomer.

98. *Oxanilic Acid, Nitric Acid (excess over 1.25 mols.) and Oxalic Acid.* Oxanilic and oxalic acids were ground together and added gradually to a large excess of nitric acid. On pouring into water, a yellowish white precipitate came down. This was filtered off and boiled with water, from which, on cooling, yellow crystals of *p*-nitroxanilic acid were deposited, melting at 209–210°. *p*-Nitroxanilic acid is soluble with difficulty in cold water but more easily in hot; it is soluble also in alcohol.

99. *The direct nitration of oxanilic acid* yields *p*-nitroxanilic acid.[4]

100. *Oxanilic Acid, Nitric Acid and Sulphuric Acid (excess over 4 mols.).* The oxanilic acid was dissolved in sulphuric acid, and nitric acid added gradually. After standing for a time, the reaction product was poured into water and an orange-red precipitate came down. This dissolved completely in boiling water, from which, on cooling, a yellow, amorphous compound separated out. It melted at 123–126°.

101. *Oxanilic Acid, Nitric Acid, and Acetic Acid (excess over 4 mols.).* Oxanilic acid was dissolved in a large excess of acetic acid. After the addition of the nitric acid the liquid was allowed to stand and, on pouring into water, a brown precipitate was ob-

---

[1] *Ann.*, 209, 367; *Ber.*, 18, 2937.
[2] *Ibid.*, 18, 2936.
[3] *N. Handw. d. Chemie* (Beilstein), 4, 265.
[4] *Ber.*, 18, 2936.

tained. This dissolved in boiling water, except for a small amount of tarry matter. Brownish crystals, melting at 145–150°, separated from the aqueous liquid.

102. *Oxanilic acid, Nitric Acid and Trichloracetic Acid.* Oxanilic acid and trichloracetic acid were ground together, and the mixture added to nitric acid, at the room temperature. On each addition of the mixture there was a reddening of the nitric acid, which, after being stirred, became yellow again. The reaction product was poured into water and gave a heavy, flocculent, yellowish-white precipitate.

2. *Experiments with Oxanilide* (Nos. 103–107).—Of the mononitro derivatives of this compound, only the meta isomer[1] appears to have been prepared. No unsymmetrical dinitro compounds are known, but descriptions of the ortho-,[2] meta-,[3] and parasymmetrical[4] dinitroanilides are to be found in the literature.

3. *Oxanilide, Nitric Acid (2.5 mols.) and Sulphuric Acid.*—Oxanilide was dissolved in sulphuric acid, and nitric acid added drop by drop, the liquid being well cooled. On pouring the reaction-product into water, filtering and drying, a yellowish-white powder was obtained. It was evidently a meta isomer because, when hydrolyzed, it gave m-nitraniline, m. p. 109–113°.

104. *Nitration of oxanilide in the presence of acetic acid* yields p-dinitroxanilide.[5]

105. *Oxanilide, Nitric Acid (2.5 mols.) and Trichloracetic Acid.* The materials were mixed in the usual manner, allowed to stand, then heated on the water bath for an hour and finally allowed to remain at the room temperature for several days. On pouring into water, a yellow precipitate came down. Glacial acetic acid extracted from this a white powder melting at 235–237°.

106. *Oxanilide and Nitric Acid (large excess over 2.5 mols.).* The anilide was added to the nitric acid at the room temperature. After standing for a few minutes, the whole mass solidified, the temperature rose, and nitrogen peroxide was evolved. After remaining over-night it was poured into water, which precipitated a yellow compound. This was filtered off, dried and extracted with glacial acetic acid. From this solution, a white powder separated m. p. 232–240°.

107. *Oxanilide, Nitric Acid (excess over 2.5 mols.) and Oxalic Acid.* The anilide and oxalic acid were ground together and added to the nitric acid at the room temperature. In a few minutes the mass solidified, the temperature rose and nitrogen peroxide was evolved. After standing over-night, water was added to the mixture, and a yellow precipitate separated.

3. *Experiments with Succinanilic Acid* (Nos. 108–112).—The ortho-,[6]

[1] *Bull. soc. chim.*, 81, 1569; *Zentr.*, 1903, I, 157.
[2] *Ann.*, 209, 369.
[3] *N. Handw. d. Chem.* (Beilstein), 4, 956.
[4] *Ann.*, 209, 366; *Ber.*, 8, 473.
[5] *Ann.*, 209, 366.
[6] *Ann.*, 292, 190; 327, 54; *Zentralbl.*, 1903, I, 1336.

meta-,[1] and paranitro[2] derivatives of this compound have all been prepared.

108. *Succinanilic Acid, Nitric Acid and Sulphuric Acid (excess over 4 mols.).* Succinanilic acid was dissolved in sulphuric acid on the water bath and then nitric acid added, the mixture being well cooled. After standing for several hours, the reaction product was poured into water, which gave a yellow precipitate. This was filtered off, dried and then extracted with hot water. On cooling, an orange-yellow compound melting at 149–164° was deposited. When hydrolyzed, it yielded *m*-nitraniline, m. p. 112–114°.

109. *Succinanilic Acid, Nitric Acid and Acetic Acid (excess over 4 mols.).* Succinanilic acid was dissolved in an excess of hot acetic acid, and nitric acid added to the solution, at the room temperature. After standing for twenty-four hours, the reaction mixture was colored brownish-red, and a brownish-yellow precipitate was obtained on pouring it into water. The crude nitration product was dissolved in boiling water, from which brown needles separated on cooling; they melted at 153–154.5°.

110. *Succinanilic Acid, Nitric Acid (excess over 1.25 mols.) and Oxalic Acid.* Succinanilic acid and oxalic acid were ground together and then gradually added to a large excess of well cooled nitric acid. If the addition is too rapid decomposition takes place. On standing over-night and pouring into water, a yellow precipitate was obtained. This was filtered off, dried and washed with a little chloroform. The residue, insoluble in chloroform, melted at 196–197° and gave *p*-nitraniline, m. p. 146–147°, on being hydrolyzed with hydrochloric acid. *p*-Nitrosuccinanilic acid is soluble in alcohol, ethyl acetate, chloroform and acetic acid; less soluble in hot water; soluble with difficulty in ether, benzene, and ligroin.

111. *Succinanilic Acid, and Nitric Acid (excess over 1.25 mols.).* Succinanilic acid was added to nitric acid at the room temperature. There was a slight decomposition of the nitric acid, and the whole mass was at once poured into water, giving a yellow precipitate.

112. *Succinanilic Acid, Nitric Acid and Trichloracetic Acid.* Succinanilic acid and trichloracetic acid were ground together, and then nitric acid thoroughly mixed with them at the room temperature. The mixture was poured into water at once and gave a small amount of an orange precipitate, together with some red, tarry matter.

4. *Experiments with Succinanil* (Nos. 113–117).—A number of chemists have investigated the ortho-[3] and para-nitro[4] derivatives of this compound, but the meta isomer does not appear to have been prepared.

113. *By direct nitration of succinanil,* ortho- and paranitrosuccinanil are obtained.[5]

114. *Succinanil, Nitric Acid and Trichloracetic Acid.* Succinanil and trichloracetic acid were ground together, then nitric acid ground with the mixture at the room tem-

---

[1] *Ann.,* 327, 54.
[2] *Ibid.,* 292, 191; 327, 55; *Zentralbl.,* 1903, I, 1336.
[3] *Ber.,* 8, 1225; *Ann.,* 209, 374; 292, 191.
[4] *Ber.,* 8, 1225; 29, 2679; *Ann.,* 209, 375; 292, 191; 327, 49 *Ann.*; *Zentr.,* 1903, I, 1336.
[5] *Ann.,* 209, 374, 375; 292, 191.

perature, and the whole allowed to stand several hours. On pouring into water, a faintly yellow precipitate was obtained, which, after being filtered and dried, melted at 156–158°. Hydrolysis with hydrochloric acid gave no nitraniline.

115. *Succinanil, Nitric Acid (excess over 1.25 mols.) and Oxalic Acid.* Succinanil and oxalic acid were ground together and added to a large excess of nitric acid. The mixture was heated on the water bath for fifteen minutes and then poured into water, when a yellow, flocculent precipitate came down. On boiling this precipitate with water and then cooling, red-brown needles melting at 150–152° were obtained. The residue, insoluble in boiling water, was dissolved in boiling alcohol, from which a brownish-yellow material deposited. It proved to be p-nitrosuccinanil, m. p. 205–207°. It is insoluble in water, slightly soluble in cold alcohol, soluble with difficulty in chloroform and boiling alcohol, ether and ligroin, but it dissolves easily in hot chloroform.

116. *Succinanil, Nitric Acid and Acetic Acid.* Succinanil was dissolved in acetic acid, nitric acid added, and the mixture heated for several hours on the water bath. On pouring into water, a chocolate-brown precipitate was deposited. Reddish-brown needles, which melted at 154–156°, separated from the filtrate.

117. *Succinanil, Nitric Acid and Sulphuric Acid.* Succinanil was dissolved in sulphuric acid and nitric acid added gradually. On pouring into water, a heavy, yellow, amorphous precipitate came down. This was boiled with water to remove unchanged succinanil. On hydrolyzing the reaction product with hydrochloric acid and neutralizing with sodium carbonate, yellow crystals of p-nitraniline (m. p. 146–148°) were obtained.

5. *Experiments with Succinanilide* (Nos. 118–120).—I have been unable to find a reference of any mononitro derivatives of this compound. The only known dinitro product appears to be the disymmetrical para isomer.[1]

118. *Succinanilide, Nitric Acid and Sulphuric Acid (excess over 4 mols.).* Succinanilide was dissolved in sulphuric acid on the water bath, nitric acid was added, and the mixture allowed to stand several days at the room temperature. On pouring into water a small quantity of a yellow-red precipitate was obtained. The crude precipitate was extracted with boiling water, from which a red, tarry compound separated on cooling. It melted at 118–136°.

119. *Succinanilide, Nitric Acid (excess over 1.25 mols.) and Oxalic Acid.* Succinanilide and oxalic acid were ground together and the mixture added gradually to an excess of cooled nitric acid. After standing for a time, the liquid was poured into water. This gave a reddish-brown precipitate.

120. *The direct nitration of succinanilide* yields succin-p-dinitranilide.[1]

6. *Experiments with Tartranilide* (Nos. 121–125).—I have been unable to find description of any nitro derivative of this compound.

121. *Tartranilide, Nitric Acid (2.5 mols.) and Sulphuric Acid.* Tartranilide and sulphuric acid were mixed, and nitric acid added to the mixture. On pouring into

[1] *Ann.*, 209, 377.

water, a yellow precipitate came down. It was boiled with water. After filtering and cooling the filtrate, a yellow product was obtained which had an indefinite melting point, but was completely melted at 191°. The portion of the nitration product insoluble in water was boiled with alcohol and filtered. On cooling, the filtrate deposited a white substance which melted at 220–240°. The residue insoluble in alcohol was dissolved in acetone. It crystallized out as a gray powder melting at 258–261°.

122. *Tartranilide, Nitric Acid (2.5 mols.) and Acetic Acid.* Tartranilide was heated with acetic acid on the water bath, and nitric acid added, after which the mixture was heated on the water bath for six hours. The solution was colored dark-red and there was a yellow, insoluble solid. On pouring into water, a yellowish-brown precipitate was obtained. This precipitate was extracted with boiling water from which a yellow compound separated on cooling. It melted and decomposed at 255–256°. At 230–235° a small amount of volatile matter sublimed from it. The residue, insoluble in boiling water, was extracted with boiling alcohol, from which a flocculent, white powder crystallized. This melted at 250–256°. The residue insoluble in boiling alcohol consisted of a fine, white powder melting at 269–271°.

123. *Tartranilide, Nitric Acid (excess over 2.5 mols.) and Oxalic Acid.* Tartranilide and oxalic acid were ground together and added gradually to a well-cooled excess of nitric acid. After a few minutes' standing, the reaction product was poured into water, which gave a yellow precipitate. This crude precipitate was extracted with boiling water, from which, on cooling, a fine, yellow compound melting at 181–185°, separated. The residue insoluble in boiling water was then extracted with boiling alcohol, from which also a yellow product crystallized out. It melted at 233–235°. The portion insoluble in boiling alcohol melted at 249–251°.

124. *Tartranilide, Nitric Acid (2.5 mols.) and Trichloracetic Acid.* Tartranilide and trichloracetic acid were ground together, and nitric acid added at the room temperature. After standing several days, the reaction product was poured into water and a brown precipitate separated out.

125. *Tartranilide and Nitric Acid (excess over 2.5 mols.).* Tartranilide was added gradually to an excess of well-cooled nitric acid. After standing a *few* minutes, the reaction product was poured into water, producing a yellow precipitate. On boiling this precipitate with water, filtering, and cooling the solution, yellow crystals, melting at 164–184°, were obtained. The residue insoluble in boiling water was boiled with alcohol, from which a voluminous compound separated on cooling; it melted and decomposed at 218–225°. The residue insoluble in boiling alcohol melted and decomposed at 236–241°. The crude nitration product was hydrolyzed by means of hydrochloric acid; the yellow crystals which separated on neutralizing the hydrochloric acid with sodium carbonate were recrystallized from methyl alcohol. They consisted of *p*-nitraniline, m. p. 144–146°.

IV. Derivatives of Tribasic Acids.

1. *Experiments with Citranilide* (Nos. 126–130).—I have failed to find any record of the preparation of nitro derivatives of this compound.

126.
Nitric and sulphuric acids gave a yellowish-brown precipitate, from which boiling water extracted a yellow, amorphous substance, melting and decomposing at 140–150°. From the residue alcohol dissolved a red tar.

127.
Nitric and acetic acids yielded a pink-white precipitate from which boiling water extracted a yellow tar. Treatment of the residue with alcohol yielded a yellowish-white substance, m. p. 193–195°.

128.
Nitric and oxalic acids gave a yellow precipitate.

129.
Nitric and trichloracetic acids formed a greenish-brown oil solidifying to yellowish-pink mass.

130. The direct *nitration of citranilide* yields trinitrocitranilide.[1]

2. *Experiments with Citrobianil* (Nos. 131–133).—

131.
Nitric acid alone gave lemon-yellow precipitate.

132.
Nitric and sulphuric acids yielded a reddish-orange or flocculent yellow precipitate.

133.
Nitric and oxalic acids gave a yellow precipitate.

C. Aromatic Compounds.

III. Derivatives of Dibasic Acids.

1. *Experiments with Phthalanilic Acid* (Nos. 134–138).—The ortho-,[2] meta-,[2] and paranitranilides[2] of phthalic acid have all been prepared.

134.
Nitric and sulphuric acids gave a brownish-red precipitate.

135.
Nitric and acetic acids yielded a greenish precipitate.

136.
Nitric and oxalic acids formed a yellowish-white crystalline substance.

137.
Nitric and trichloracetic acids gave a white precipitate.

138.
Nitric acid alone yielded brownish-red and pale-yellow crystals.

2. *Experiments with Phthalanil* (Nos. 139–143).—The ortho-,[3] meta-,[4] and paranitranils[5] of phthalic acid have all been prepared.

139. *Phthalanil and Nitric Acid* (*excess over 1.25 mols.*). Phthalanil was added gradually to the nitric acid, a white, powdery precipitate being thrown down. After a few moments' standing, the mixture solidified. It was treated with water, which gave a white compound. This was filtered, dried and extracted with alcohol, from which a flocculent, white substance was deposited. It melted at 183–185°.

[1] *Ber.*, **21**, 666.
[2] *Ann.*, **327**, 55; *Zentr.*, 1903, I, 1336.
[3] *Ber.*, **28**, 1210.
[4] *Ibid.*, **11**, 2261; **27**, 3430; **28**, 941; **28**, 1119.
[5] *Ibid.*, **27**, 3430; **28**, 1119; *Zentralbl.*, 1903, 1325.

The residue insoluble in alcohol was washed, successively, with boiling xylene and boiling acetic acid. The xylene extract, on cooling, gave a white, flocculent compound melting at 256–258°. From the acetic acid separated fine, white crystals melting at 264–266°. The residue, after treatment with the alcohol, xylene and acetic acid, consisted of a fine, white powder melting at 258–260°. The product from the acetic acid solution was identified as being p-nitrophthalanil.

140. *Phthalanil, Nitric Acid and Sulphuric Acid (excess over 4 mols.).* Phthalanil was dissolved in an excess of sulphuric acid, and nitric acid added carefully, the liquid being well cooled. After standing over-night, the reaction mixture was poured into water. A yellow precipitate was formed. A hot alcoholic extract of this crude material gave, on cooling, spherical aggregates of small, red crystals which melted and decomposed at 165–175°.

141. *Phthalanil, Nitric Acid (excess over 1.25 mols.) and Oxalic Acid.* Phthalanil and oxalic acid were ground together and added to well-cooled nitric acid. The mixture speedily changed to a white solid. This was poured into water, filtered, dried and washed, successively, with boiling xylene, boiling alcohol and boiling acetic acid. The residue was then dried; it melted at 262–264°, showing that it was the paranitro derivative. The precipitate from the alcoholic extract was colored brownish-yellow, and melted at 152–154°. White crystals melting at 262–265°, were obtained from the acetic acid solution. From the xylene, a white compound, melting at 200–205°, separated.

142. *Phthalanil, Nitric Acid and Acetic Acid (excess over 4 mols.).* Phthalanil was dissolved in acetic acid and nitric acid added at the temperature of the boiling water bath. The mixture was heated until it gave a precipitate on adding a little of it to water. The compound so obtained was yellowish-white; it was extracted with alcohol, from which a flocculent, white substance, melting at 205–208°, separated. The residue insoluble in alcohol consisted of beautiful, white crystals melting at 205–208°.

143. *Phthalanil, Nitric Acid and Trichloracetic Acid.* Phthalanil and trichloracetic acid were ground together, and the nitric acid added at the room temperature. The reaction mixture was then poured immediately into water. A white precipitate was formed.

Summary.

A considerable number of N-substituted aniline derivatives have been nitrated in the presence of sulphuric acid, acetic acid, oxalic acid, and trichloracetic acid.

The use of oxalic acid and trichloracetic acid in this connection is new.

The position assumed by the entering nitro-group is influenced by the N-substituent.

The position assumed by the entering nitro-group is also influenced by the nature of the admixed acid.

Various hydrolyses of the nitration products have been made.

I. Monalkyl Derivatives.

All the nitration experiments with compounds of this class yielded tars. Metanitro derivatives had been obtained previously by other chemists from both methyl- and ethylaniline by nitrating in the presence of sulphuric acid (Expts. 20–24).

II. Dialkyl Derivatives.

The formation of tar was the general result of the nitration of the members of this class. However, in nitrating dimethyl- and diethylaniline in the presence of sulphuric acid, *metanitro* derivatives have been produced in both cases (Expts. 25 and 31).

The nitration of dimethylaniline in the presence of acetic acid has been found to yield *p*-nitromethylaniline (Expt. 26). In nitrating dimethylaniline in the presence of a mixture of oxalic and acetic acids, I obtained *p*-nitrodimethylaniline (Expt. 30).

I have also prepared several new compounds, notably one from diphenylamine, the nature of which it is hoped to elucidate later.

III. Derivatives of Monobasic Aliphatic Acids.

Formanilide, by direct nitration, gave the *paranitro* derivative (Exp. 46), which was also obtained in the presence of sulphuric acid (Expt. 42).

Acetanilide, by direct nitration, yielded a mixture of *ortho-* and *paranitro derivatives* (Expt. 50). In the presence of sulphuric acid, *metanitro acetanilide* was obtained (Expt. 47). The oxalic and trichloracetic acid nitrations both gave *paranitro derivatives* (Expts. 48, 49).

The nitrations of trichloracetanilide, propanilide and stearanilide gave products which have not yet been identified.

IV. Derivatives of Monobasic Aromatic Acids.

Benzanilide yields a mixture of *ortho-*, *meta-*, and *paranitro derivatives* by direct nitration (Expt. 72). With sulphuric acid, *para*nitrobenzanilide was obtained (Expt. 67). Acetic acid nitration gave *meta*-nitrobenzanilide (Expt. 68). A mixture of oxalic and acetic acids gave the *para*nitro derivative (Expt. 69).

None of the nitration products of *m*-brombenzanilide, benzenesulphanilide, *o*-tolylsulphanilide, phenylacetanilide or picranilide have, as yet, been identified, owing to causes beyond my control.

Derivatives of Aliphatic Dibasic Acids.

By direct nitration (Exp. 99) and also in the presence of oxalic acid (Exp. 98), oxanilic acid gave the *paranitro* derivative.

Oxanilide gave the *metanitro* derivative by nitration in the presence of sulphuric acid (Exp. 103) and the *paranitro* derivative by nitration in the presence of acetic acid (Exp. 104). Succinanilic acid, by nitration in the presence of sulphuric acid (Exp. 108), yielded *metanitrosuccinanilic* acid, whereas nitration in the presence of oxalic acid gave the *paranitro* derivative (Exp. 110). Direct nitration of succinanil gave a mixture of *ortho-* and *paranitro* derivatives (Exp. 113). With sulphuric acid (Exp. 117), the *paranitro* derivative was obtained. Oxalic acid nitration of succinanil (Exp. 115) gave the *paranitro* derivative. The symmetrical *paradinitro* derivative of succinanilide was obtained by direct nitration (Exp. 120). Tartranilide gave the *paranitro* derivative by direct nitration (Exp. 125). The products obtained from the remaining nitrations have not, as yet, been identified.

Derivatives of Aromatic Dibasic Acids.

Phthalanil, both by direct nitration (Exp. 139) and by nitration in the presence of oxalic acid (Exp. 141), yields *paranitro*phthalanil. The other nitration products of phthalanil and those of phthalanilic acid have not, hitherto, been identified.

Derivatives of Aliphatic Tribasic Acids.

The direct nitration of citranilide gave a trinitro derivative (Exp. 130). The other new nitration products have not been identified.

For convenience of reference, I have embodied my results in the following table, but I have not included in it the work comprised in the large number of experiments in which I obtained unidentified compounds.

Substance.	Direct nitration.	Nitric and oxalic acids.	Nitric and acetic acids.	Nitric and sulphuric acids.	Nitric and trichloracetic acids.
Methylaniline	..	..	..	m-	..
Ethylaniline	..	..	..	m- and little p-	..
Dimethylaniline	..	p-[1]	p-	m-	..
Diethylaniline	..	..	..	m- and p-	..
Benzalaniline	Hydrolyzed to benzaldehyde and aniline.				
Formanilide	p-	..	..	p-	..
Acetanilide	p- and o-	p-	No reaction	m-	p-

[1] Formed with oxalic, acetic and nitric acids.

Substance.	Direct nitration.	Nitric and oxalic acids.	Nitric and acetic acids.	Nitric and sulphuric acids.	Nitric and trichloracetic acids.
Benzanilide	o-, m- and p-	p-[1]	m-	p-	..
Oxanilic acid	p-	p-	..	..	..
Oxanilide	..	..	p-	m-	..
Succinanilic acid	..	p-	..	m-	..
Succinanil	o- and p-	p-	..	p-	..
Succinanilide	p-	..	..	..	..
Tartranilide	p-	..	..	..	..
Citranilide	m-	..	..	..	..
Phthalanil	p-	p-	..	..	..

It should be pointed out that the products mentioned in the table are the *chief* substances formed during the experiments, but not necessarily the only ones. I have not attempted to detect *traces* of isomers, but, in so far as time has permitted, I have isolated the essential products of the reactions.

General Discussion of Results.

Until the constitution of the numerous new compounds which I have prepared has been worked out more fully, it would be premature to offer any dogmatic statements regarding the influence of the nature of the *N*-substituent on the course of nitration. I desire, however, to consider briefly the question of the influence of the admixed acids. *Direct* nitration, in all cases in which the products were identified, yielded either the *paranitro* derivative or a mixture of *ortho-* and *paranitro* derivatives, except in the case of benzanilide, which also yielded some *metanitro* derivative.

Nitration in the presence of sulphuric acid yields either the *metanitro* derivative exclusively, or a greater percentage of the *meta* product.

Oxalic acid seems to exert no influence on the course of the nitration, because in all cases except, perhaps, succinanil, the products were the same as those obtained from direct nitration. This, as already suggested, is probably due to the sparing solubility of oxalic acid in nitric acid, in consequence of which the active mass of the former was evidently too small for it to exert any appreciable influence. This suggestion is confirmed by the fact that in the case of benzanilide, when the oxalic acid was dissolved in acetic acid, *benzparanitranilide* is produced, whereas acetic acid without the oxalic acid leads to the formation of the *meta* compound, and nitric acid alone yields all three isomers.

The products from the trichloracetic acid nitrations have not, as yet,

[1] Formed with oxalic, acetic and nitric acids.

been identified. Reactions, however, seem to take place even more readily in the presence of this acid than in the case of sulphuric acid. It is hoped to study later the influence of these acids and, possibly, of other substances on the formation of such compounds as nitramines, i. e., to ascertain whether their presence favors the nitration of the NHRR' group rather than that of the benzene nucleus. It is quite evident, however, that the nature of the acid which is mixed with the nitric acid exerts a definite directive influence on the *position assumed by the entrant nitro group*.[1]

As will be evident from the foregoing pages, a considerable number of products have been obtained which could not be identified with known compounds because only a rather limited number of N-substituted anilines have been prepared. The simplest way that suggested itself was to hydrolyze my new substances with acids or alkalies and purify and isolate the resulting nitraniline or mixture of nitranilines. Concentrated hydrochloric acid, alcoholic hydrochloric acid, aqueous and alcoholic solutions of alkali hydroxides, sulphuric acid, and also barium hydroxide were used as the hydrolyzing agents, the experiments being carried out at the temperature of the boiling water bath. In a few cases, where the hydrolyses were not successful, attempts were made to reduce the substances with tin and hydrochloric acid and also with zinc dust and acetic acid. These experiments were essentially of a preliminary nature and were not completed.

It appears to me desirable to discuss, at this point, two subjects which have naturally been thrust very much on my attention during the progress of my work. The first concerns the correct representation of disubstitution products of benzene; the second, the mechanism of substitution.

The various plane formulae for benzene which have been proposed from time to time need not be referred to further, because benzene, like most other substances, exists in three, and not in one dimension! Of spatial formulae, the variety is not so great, but the fate of the ones brought forward has not been much happier than that of those existing in a single plane. The chief objection to the current formulae, from the point of view of substitution, is that the para positions are shown as being the most widely separated, whereas, as a matter of experimental fact, strongly negative groups take up the meta positions. We know, however, that bodies

[1] Cf. Bishop Tingle and Blanck: *Am. Chem. J.*, 36, 607 (1906).

charged with electricity of the same sign tend to repel one another and that, in general, in chemistry, it is compounds of opposite electrical sign which combine most easily. Consequently, it would be expected that two strongly negative groups would tend to take up positions in the molecule as far apart as possible. The question is, therefore, can a formula for benzene be devised which will have the meta positions further removed from one another in space than are the para positions? To prevent misapprehension, it may be as well to state expressly that the above problem does not contain any suggestion opposed to the substituents in the meta position being separated by one carbon atom and those in the para by two; that these are the relative positions of the isomers in question is, of course, established by the firmest experimental evidence. This separation by one or two carbon atoms, however, is perfectly compatible with the closer proximity of the substituents in the latter than in the former case.

About two years ago Barlow and Pope[1] brought forward a new spatial conception of benzene, in which they represent its molecule as built up in layers.

According to this "the production of a monosubstitution derivative, C_6H_5X, necessitates the replacement of one hydrogen sphere in each alternate layer .... by the substituting group X; the introduction of a second group X to give the derivative $C_6H_4X_2$ may be brought about in two generally distinct ways: the second group X may enter the column in the same layers in which the first group was introduced, leaving the alternate layers still unsubstituted, and in this case a *metadi*-derivative alone will be found; or the second group X may be introduced into the alternate layers, into which the X group did not originally enter, and then an *ortho-* or *paradi*-derivative, or both, will be found. A complete geometrical difference in kind thus exists between the derivative of the 1 : 3-*di*-derivative and that of 1 : 2- and 1 : 4-isomers; this is wholly in harmony with the observed chemical facts."

The results obtained by me are fully and satisfactorily accounted for by this new formula of Barlow and Pope for benzene. Indeed, it may be said of it that, for the first time, a formula has been proposed which can account spatially for the formation, under the influence of *negative* groups, of meta disubstitution products instead of *para* derivatives. Should objec-

[1] *J. Chem. Soc.*, **89**, 1697 (1906).

tions be raised to Barlow and Pope's formula on the ground that it is static, for instance (which I am far from wishing to do), I think that it might be possible to suggest a spatal formula which would be free from this objection and which would, at the same time, meet the requirements mentioned above. The conception of Barlow and Pope is, however, so valuable on account of its correlation of chemical and crystallographic properties, that it is sincerely to be hoped that it will be found fully adequate for all other purposes.

Turning now to the question of the mechanism of substitution and confining our attention to nitration, there is the well-known fact that dilute nitric acid oxidizes but does not nitrate, the action being essentially reversed in the case of concentrated acid. The former consists, of course, of nitric acid molecules and of the ions H^+ and NO_3^-, whereas these ions are relatively scarce in the highly concentrated acid which, in addition to molecular nitric acid, contains its *ordinary—not electrolytic—*dissociation products, $HO + NO_2$. When the equilibrium is disturbed, the dissociated hydroxyl radicles doubtless combine to form water and oxygen. The question thus arises, does nitration occur essentially as the result of the action of —NO_2 radicles, or is it caused by molecular nitric acid? There is some evidence to show that the nitration of acetanilide, for example, is not retarded to any material extent by the presence of carbamide, a result which, I think, is in conflict with the idea that the —NO_2 radicles, or nitrous acid, are the active nitrating agents.

Accepting, provisionally, the idea that nitration is the result of the action of molecular nitric acid, nitration must be preceded by addition, which might be thought of as taking place, in the case of benzene for instance, in the manner represented by one of the following expressions:

(1) $C_6H_5 — + — H + HNO_3 \longrightarrow ON(OH)_2C_6H_5 \longrightarrow H_2O + C_6H_5NO_2$.
(2) $C_6H_6 + HNO_3 \longrightarrow ON(OH)_2C_6H_5 \longrightarrow H_2O + C_6H_5NO_2$.

For the sake of simplicity the hypothetical intermediate compound is represented as being identical in the two cases; actually, it might not be so.

Of these rival views, I decidedly favor the second, because there is nothing at all strange in the suggestion of the direct combination of two such highly unsaturated molecules as those of benzene and nitric acid.

Against the idea represented in the first of the above expressions, that benzene is dissociated into phenyl and hydrogen, a number of considerations may be urged. What is the nature of this dissociation?

Obviously it is not electrolytic, because benzene is not a conductor of electricity. Obviously, also, it is not dissociation in the ordinary sense of the term, as applied to phosphorus pentachloride, for example, because, when boiled, benzene does not evolve hydrogen. The fact that benzene does yield a small proportion of diphenyl and hydrogen when passed through a tube heated to redness cannot be relied on as an argument, because of the difference in the physical conditions prevailing in the cases under consideration. Of course, it may be said that if there is appreciable dissociation at a red heat there must be *some* dissociation, however little, at the ordinary temperature. This statement, even if correct metaphysically, can have no practical importance until it is shown, by experiment, that the dissociation in question actually occurs at the temperature indicated. In other words, it relegates the question to the class occupied by "insoluble" substances, or by compounds which react with infinite slowness; they are of no practical importance so long as life itself is limited.

Finally, it may be pointed out that the recent well-known and brilliant work of Baly and his colleagues on the optical properties of benzene and allied compounds is entirely against there being such a dissociation. If, in spite of these considerations and of others which could be mentioned, the idea of dissociation is still retained for the reaction under consideration, we have a right to ask that it be named and defined, for it is evidently of an entirely new and strange variety.

If the considerations advanced in the preceding paragraphs are correct, we are driven to regard substitution as essentially an addition phenomenon, a view which has been discussed at some length by H. E. Armstrong in a series of papers.[1] Without committing myself to agreement with the details of his scheme of reactions, parts of which, indeed, are rather vague, yet, in general, I join him in regarding substitution as being preceded by addition.

With regard to the special case of aniline, the question arises, Does this addition occur in the nucleus, as in the nitration of benzene, or is the substituted amino group the point of attack? I believe that my experiments with aniline and nitric acid furnish ground for at least a tentative answer to this question. In these experiments, aniline nitrate is first formed, excess of concentrated nitric acid changes this into a colored,

[1] *Vide*, especially *Proc. Chem. Soc.*, **7**, 89 (1891).

unstable compound which is reconverted into the nitrate on the addition of water. Here, then, the amino group is attacked first and, apparently, the next stage in the change is the dehydration of this nitrate, leading to the production of a deeply colored body. I believe that it is best to regard this latter substance as being a "nitramine," $C_6H_5NHNO_2$, or, possibly, a nitrate of this substance, such as $C_6H_5NH_2(NO_2)ONO_2$. Although such a representation may serve as a noncommittal formula for the compound, it is not satisfactory because it fails entirely to account for the color. In such substances as the one under consideration Hantzsch[1] has shown; very clearly; that color is associated with a cyclic structure. In analogy with the nitrophenols, I suggest the formula,

$\underset{}{\text{[benzene ring with -NH and -NOOH substituents]}}$, as most probably representing the constitution of the

colored compound. The choice of the meta linkage is, of course, purely arbitrary. The formula given accounts not only for the color of the substance, but explains the ease with which it passes into aniline nitrate by the addition of water, whereas, on the other hand, it also indicates that it should change readily into a nitraniline. Investigations regarding this last point are about to be made.

In the case of the N-substituted anilines where nitraniline derivatives are obtained with ease, I feel justified, at present, in regarding their formation as being due, primarily, to an addition of nitric acid to the nucleus. In cases where nitrosamines are the chief products, it is evident that the substituted amine group participates in the change. In all probability, in most cases, both reactions occur simultaneously, the experimental conditions, including the nitrating material, and the nature of the N-substituents determining which shall be the predominant reaction in any given instance. The question of the "protection" of the amino group has been already discussed in another connection in this dissertation.[2]

Work is being continued at the McMaster University, under the direction of Professor Tingle, in the hope that it may throw further light on the very important and highly interesting questions referred to above. The present contribution can be regarded only as a preliminary survey of some of the ground which it will be necessary to explore before anything like positive conclusions can be reached.

[1] *Ber.*, 39, 1084, 3072; 40, 1556.
[2] Cf. Bishop Tingle and Blanck: *Am. Chem. J.*, 36, 607 (1906); *Ibid.*, 30, 1395.

BIOGRAPHICAL.

Fred C. Blanck was born in Baltimore, Maryland, on October 14, 1881. His preparation for college was received in the Baltimore City College. He entered upon the college course in the Johns Hopkins University in October, 1900, and received the degree of Bachelor of Arts in June, 1903. Since then he has been enrolled in the Johns Hopkins University as a graduate student in chemistry, his subordinate subjects being physical chemistry and mineralogy.

Printed by Libri Plureos GmbH in Hamburg, Germany